JOURNEY THROUGH
BRAZIL

LIZ GOGERLY
&
ROB HUNT

W
FRANKLIN WATTS
LONDON•SYDNEY

Franklin Watts
Published in Great Britain in 2017 by The Watts Publishing Group

Credits
Editor in Chief: John Miles
Series Editor: Amy Stephenson
Series Designer: Emma DeBanks
Picture Researcher: Diana Morris

Picture Credits: Affoto/Dreamstime: 25b. agefotostock/Superstock: 12c. Aguina/Dreamstime: 29t. Alexandrpeers/Dreamstime: 7tc. Edite Antmann/Dreamstime: 7br. Ivan Barreto/Dreamstime: 19c. Bevanward/Dreamstime: 7br, 21t. Biosphoto/Superstock: 13b. Rodrigo Silveira Camargo Wikimedia Commons: 4l. Valter Campanato: 20. Patrick K Campbell/Shutterstock: 9c. cellistka/Shutterstock: 7bl. marcel clemens/Shutterstock: 19t. André Costa/Dreamstime: 18t. Stefano Ember/Shutterstock: 9t. Eye Ubiquitous/Superstock: 13t. Sylvain Grandadam/Robert Harding PL: 21b. gst/Shutterstock: 7bcr. guentermanaus/Shutterstock: 14. Jorg Hackemann/Dreamstime: 21c. Imago/Photoshot: 27b. isarescheewin/Shutterstock: 7tl. Eric Isselee/Shutterstock: 7bcb. KlaraLuna.com: 4r. Sergey Korotkov/Dreamstime: 6tl, 8. Lazyllama/Dreamstime: 22. Anke Leifeld/Dreamstime: 15c. Yadid Levy/RHPL/Superstock: 17c. Lunamarina/Dreamstime: 7tr. luoman/istockphoto: 15b. Johnny Lye/Shutterstock: 1, 6cr, 15t. Marcus VDT/Shutterstock: 9b. Alessio Moiola/Dreamstime: 5b, 16b, 17t. Lorena Mossa:10. Felipe Oliveira/Dreamstime: 6b, 17b. Olyina/Shutterstock: 24b. ostill/Shutterstock: front cover. Paura/Dreamstime: 5t. Pixattitude/Dreamstime: 19b. Luiz C Ribero/Shutterstock: 16c. Rita77/Dreamstime: 23b. Celso Pupo Rodrigues Dreamstime: 3, 18b. William Rodrigues dos Santos/Dreamstime: 27t. Marc Schwar/Robert Harding PL: 29b. Rainer W Schlegelmilch/Getty Images: 25t. Seregam/Shutterstock: 7cl. sfmthd/Dreamstime: 23c. Valery Sharifulin/Photoshot: 28. Snehitdesign /Dreamstime: 24-25, 26. Sohns/Okapia/Robert Harding PL: 11t. tereez/Shutterstock: 7cr. Richard Thomas Dreamstime: 7bc. Oscar Espinosa Villegas/Dreamstime: 12b. Valentyn Volkov/Shutterstock: 7bcl. wpid photo: 6cl, 11c. Zaramira/Dreamstime: 23t S Zelfit/Shutterstock: 7c.

Dewey number: 981
ISBN: 978 1 4451 3670 7

Printed in China

Franklin Watts
An imprint of
Hachette Children's Group
Part of The Watts Publishing Group
Carmelite House
50 Victoria Embankment
London EC4Y 0DZ

An Hachette UK Company
www.hachette.co.uk

www.franklinwatts.co.uk

CONTENTS

Belo Brasil 4

Journey planner 6

Porto Alegre to Iguaçu Falls 8

Pantanal Paradise 10

Rio Branco 12

The amazing rainforest 14

Brazil's beautiful beaches............................... 16

Beautiful Bahia 18

Brasília 20

Rio de Janeiro 22

São Paulo 24

São Bernardo do Campo to Santos............... 26

Southern Brazil... 28

Glossary/Websites/Find out more 30

Index 32

BELO BRASIL

Welcome to *'belo'* (beautiful) Brazil, the largest country in South America and the fifth biggest country in the world. People from overseas sometimes stereotype the country as obsessed with beach-life, football and generally having a good time, but Brazil is a huge and varied country and diverse in many ways.

Brazil's history in brief

Humans have lived in Brazil for at least 11,000 years, and it was estimated to have a population of anywhere between one and 11 million when the first Portuguese explorer, Pedro Cabral, landed in 1500. The Portuguese originally called it *Ilha de Vera Cruz* (Island of the True Cross), but eventually it became known by its nickname *Terra do Brasil*, probably because of the trade in the valuable brazilwood that grew on the coast.

▲ The brazilwood is a species of tree that is native to Brazil.

Brazilwood

As well as being useful for making items such as bows for stringed instruments, brazilwood provides a very valuable red dye. In fact, the name 'brasil' comes from the Portuguese word *brasa* meaning deep-red, like the glowing embers of a fire. Deforestation and illegal logging for export have brought brazilwood to the edge of extinction.

▼ Brazilwood produces a beautiful rich, red dye.

Southern seasons

Most of Brazil is in the southern hemisphere, so the summer months are between December and April. There is a brief autumn and then winter lasts from June to September, before spring returns. Most of Brazil has a tropical climate with lots of warm and wet weather. However, parts of Brazil receive almost no rainfall, whilst others are cold enough for snow.

Multi-ethnic make-up

It is believed that South America was one of the last continents to become inhabited by humans! Today, Brazil has one of the most diverse populations on the planet, with many of its inhabitants able to claim a mix of Asian, African, European and indigenous (native) heritage. In Brazil you'll hear many different languages spoken, but the official language is Portuguese.

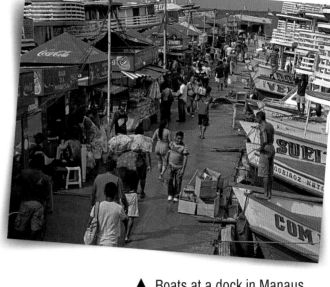

▲ Boats at a dock in Manaus transport people and goods along the River Negro.

Big in Brazil

Brazil is big! It borders ten other countries, stretches through three time zones and has a coastline of 7,491 km! Fortunately for you it has lots of airports, a really good bus system, and one of the most extensive river systems, to help you on your journey.

▼ The spectacular sand dunes at the Lençóis Maranhenses National Park may look like a desert, but the area receives too much rain to be called a true desert.

Top tips for travellers

- ➲ The 'OK' sign with your fingers is very rude in Brazil so don't use it.
- ➲ Men shake hands with each other when they first meet, while women usually kiss on the cheeks.
- ➲ It's okay to stare – everyone loves to look at everyone in Brazil, so don't forget to join in!
- ➲ Get vaccinated against tropical diseases like yellow fever and take medication to help prevent malaria at least a month before you travel.

JOURNEY PLANNER

VENEZUELA

B

COLUMBIA

PERU

Leticia

Mâncio Lima

Sena Maduireira

Moca do Acre

Humatia

Chico Mendes Park

Rio Branco

Cannd do Jam

Xapuri

Nova Mamore

BOLIVIA

YOUR JOURNEY

1

2

South Pacific Ocean

3

CHILE

4

ARGENTINA

KEY

— your route around Brazil

----- flight / boat trip

— river

— road

★ capital city

GUYANA

FRENCH
GUINEA

SURIName

North Atlantic

Fernando de
Noronha

4

*Parque Nacional
Montanhas*

Macapa ◎

Ilha de Marajó

Belèm

São Luis

*Parque Nacional da
Amazônia*

3

Santarém

Manaus

Fordlândia

Altamira

*Lençóis
Maranhenses
National Park*

Parnaíba

Fortaleza

Itaituba

Marabá

Teresina

Natal

Parauapebas

Araguanina

Picos

João Pessoa

Sinop

Juazeiro do Norte

Recife

Palmas

Petrolina

Maceló

*Chapada
Diamantina*

Aracaju

Barreiras

Vale da Lua

Salvador

Brasília **5**

Itabuna

Ilhéus

South Atlantic

Cuiabá

Itaituba

Rondonópolis

Goiânia

Corumbá

Uberlândia

Belo Horizonte

Campo Grande

Araçatuba

Ouro Preto

PARAGUAY

Pres. Prudente

Rio de Janeiro

**Vila
Velha**

Pedro Juan
Caballero

São Paulo

São Vicente

Santos

Ciudad del Este
Iguaçu Falls

*Iguaçu
National Park*

Curitiba

1

Joinville

6

Florianópolis

São Joaquim

Laguna

Uruguaiana

Santa Maria

Porto Alegre

URUGUAY

Rio Grande

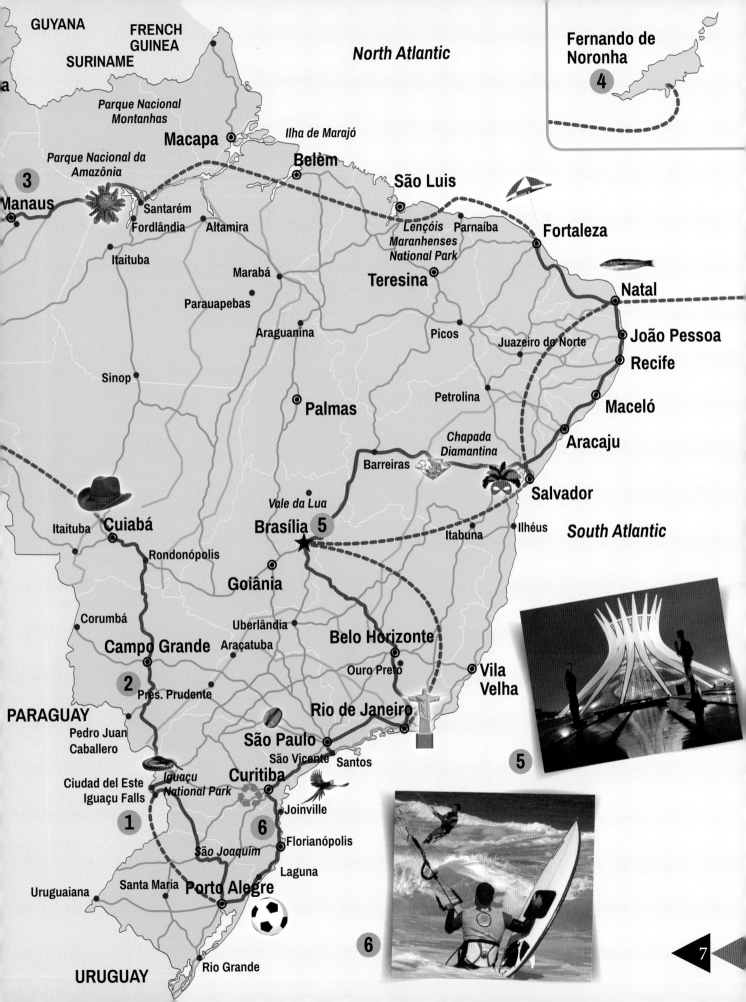

5

6

7

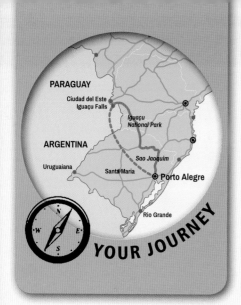

PORTO ALEGRE TO IGUAÇU FALLS

Fly into Porto Alegre, the largest city in the south, to kick off your trip. It played host to some of the football games in the 2014 World Cup. From here take a bus or plane to the Iguaçu Falls. It will take over 13 hours by bus, but a plane will get you there in just under two hours.

A wonder of nature

Iguaçu means 'big water' in the local language and the Iguaçu Falls are in a subtropical rainforest on the border between Brazil and Argentina. Iguaçu isn't the tallest waterfall in the world, but the volume of water flowing over its approximately 275 individual falls, means it more than lives up to its name. The falls are not one huge drop, like the Angel Falls in Venezuela, they are actually a series of cascades. The most famous part is called the Devil's Throat. It is a U-shaped chasm that takes about half of the river's volume and, as long as you don't mind getting soaked, you can take a speedboat ride right underneath it.

▼ The Iguaçu falls were formed by volcanic activity around 100 million years ago.

▲ The spillways at the Itaipu dam divert excess water away from the power-generating part of the dam.

Brazilian powerhouse

A short car ride, or a long walk, up river, brings you to the Itaipu Hydroelectric Dam on the Paraná River. The dam is 7,235 metres long and is the largest operating hydroelectricity-producing facility in the world, producing up to 98 billion kWh of energy per year. It supplied Paraguay with about 75 per cent of its power and Brazil with about 17 per cent of its electricity in 2013. Unfortunately, when the dam was built it created a huge reservoir, which totally submerged the world's greatest waterfall, the Guaíra Falls. These falls were over seven times bigger than the Iguaçu Falls.

▲ The green anaconda is the world's heaviest snake.

Giant rodents and spectacular snakes

The Iguaçu National Park has a wide diversity of animals. There are exotic birds like the harpy eagle and the toucan, and there are endangered species like the jaguar and the tapir. The park is also home to the world's largest rodent – the capybara. Unfortunately for the capybara, it is also home to one of the world's biggest snakes – the green anaconda, a creature more than capable of gobbling up a rodent the size of a small pig.

► The obelisk at Triple Frontier is not far from the Itaipu dam. This multi-coloured monument marks where the borders of Argentina, Brazil and Paraguay meet.

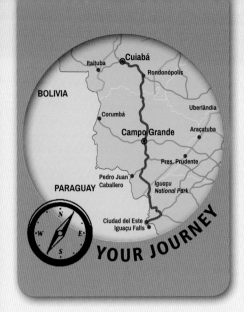

YOUR JOURNEY

PANTANAL PARADISE

All aboard the bus to the world's largest tropical wetland area! It takes 14 hours by road from the city of Foz do Iguaçu to Campo Grande – the southern gateway to the Pantanal. Brazilian buses can be very comfortable, with larger than average reclining seats and they often have toilets on board.

Gateway to the Pantanal

The Pantanal is a huge, basin-shaped area of land, covered by the water that runs off from rivers and the higher land around it. Campo Grande is probably the best place to stay before you explore this region and tours of the Pantanal can be arranged in the city. Before you head into the wetlands, take some time to enjoy the indigenous fair in the town square. You'll find decorative items such as jewellery or musical instruments skilfully crafted by the local people out of natural materials like coconut, seeds or wood.

You may be lucky enough to visit the completed Aquário do Pantanal (Pantanal Aquarium). The enormous bullet-shaped building has been under construction since 2011 and when it's finished it will be the largest freshwater aquarium in the world.

▲ A local craftsman carves wooden boats to sell at the fair.

► A cowboy rides his horse through deep water in the Pantanal wetlands.

Wild and wonderful

The name Pantanal comes from the Portuguese word *pântano*, which means swamp or wetland. The Pantanal is about the size of Great Britain and packed with animal and plant life. It's not as bio-diverse as the Amazon rainforest but you will have a better chance of seeing some exotic creatures and rare birdlife because the vegetation is less dense and far easier to explore.

Try to spot jaguars, pumas or some of the 700 or so birds that live in the Pantanal, including the world's largest parrot, the hyacinth macaw. Enjoy the daily dramas of primates such as red howler monkeys and marmosets. And, at the water's edge watch out for caiman and giant water otters. Finally, look out – there really are piranhas and vampire bats about!

Cowboy country

Your ecological encounters end when you enter the modern city of Cuiabá. This city was founded after the discovery of gold in the area in the early 18th century. It is now more famous for cattle and cowboys – known in this part of the world as gauchos (see above). If you want to buy proper cowboy boots and hats then Cuiabá is the place.

▲ A drive along the Transpantaneira can mean a bumpy ride!

Car, boat or horse?

How you travel around the Pantanal depends on the season – if it's dry you can use a four-wheel drive or even a horse. As soon as the six-month rainy season starts you'll need a boat or canoe to get to some of the more interesting places. If the weather is reasonable you can travel along the Transpantaneira highway to Cuiabá. It's called a 'highway' but it is really a 146 km-dirt-track with over 120 wooden bridges – some of them rather rickety!

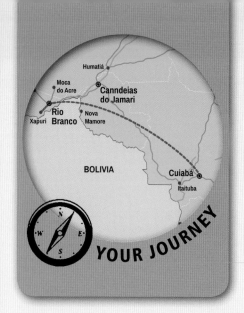

YOUR JOURNEY

RIO BRANCO

The flight from Cuiabá to Rio Branco in the state of Acre takes nearly four hours. The city of Rio Branco (Portuguese for 'white river') is built along the River Acre. It has a tropical monsoon climate making it very wet with a short dry season. You won't meet many other travellers in this remote area, which is surrounded by the Amazon rainforest.

Rubber boom town

The River Acre is one of many tributaries of the River Amazon, which criss-cross the Amazon Basin. The Amazon rainforest covers this whole area and is the only place in the world where rubber trees grow naturally in the wild. Rio Branco was founded in 1882 by rubber tappers, the people who cut into the rubber trees to extract the latex that is used to make rubber. At the time, Rio Branco was part of Bolivia but in 1903 it was made part of Brazil by law. Today, you can take a tour of a rubber plantation, watch latex being extracted from trees and find out more about how rubber is used.

▼ Milky-white latex from a rubber tree.

▼ A wet, tropical climate makes Acre a region of lush vegetation.

Hundreds of people attended Chico Mendes' funeral in 1988.

Early eco warrior

At Xapuri, near Rio Branco, you can visit the home of one of Brazil's national heroes, Chico Mendes (1944–1988). He was born into a family of rubber tappers and became one himself. He realised that rubber tapping in the area was destroying the rainforest, so he led campaigns to protect it and the people who worked in the area. At Chico Mendes Park you can find out more about this inspiring environmental leader. Sadly he was assassinated in 1988 by ranchers who wanted to chop down the rainforest to graze their cattle. Luckily, Mendes' campaigns helped to raise awareness and now a third of the state's rainforest is protected.

Highway to the Pacific

In the future you may be able to reach this isolated area by road. Work on the Interoceanic Highway, which connects Rio Branco to several ports in Peru, is underway. It crosses the Andes mountains and provides a gateway to the Pacific Ocean. The new road will improve trade and bring economic benefits. Travellers may expect to see more soya production and cattle ranchers in the area. Many people are concerned that the road will damage more areas of the rainforest.

Indigenous people

It is estimated that when Europeans arrived in Brazil in the 16th century, there were several million indigenous people living in tribes across the country. Unfortunately, they had no resistance to European diseases like measles, and many died out. Others were forced to work in the rubber trade and were killed if they tried to resist. There are still a few hundred thousand indigenous people in Brazil. Some tribes avoid all contact with 'civilisation' and Brazil is thought to have more of these tribes than any other country in the world.

A young member of the Kaxinawá tribe from Acre.

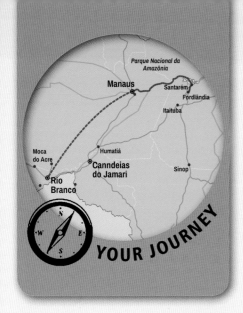

YOUR JOURNEY

THE AMAZING RAINFOREST

Unless you want to spend days in a boat, the only way to get to the remote city of Manaus is by air. It is the largest city in the Amazon Basin and is a busy city, surrounded by rainforest. From Manaus you will take a boat along the river towards Santarém where the Amazon and the Tapajós rivers meet. Keep your eyes open for the curious pink Amazon river dolphin...

Manaus

Before you venture down the River Amazon, you must sample the city whose inhabitants were once so wealthy that it was rumoured they gave their horses champagne to drink. The rubber industry brought great wealth, which disappeared when synthetic rubber was developed. Visit the impressive Teatro Amazonas, an opera house built in 1895 from materials imported, at great expense, from as far away as Germany, Scotland and Italy. The original driveway was made of local rubber to reduce the noise from the horses and carriages.

▼ The 36,000 decorated ceramic tiles that cover the dome of the Teatro Amazonas are in the colours of the Brazilian flag (green, yellow and blue).

▶ The River Amazon winds its way through dense tropical rainforest.

The River Amazon

The only way to travel long distances, at ground level, in this part of the world is by boat, due to the dense rainforest. The River Amazon is the world's second longest river after the Nile (Amazon: 6,519 km, Nile: 6,695 km) but it is by far the biggest when judged by 'discharge'. Discharge is the geographical term for the amount of water that flows. The Amazon flows at a rate of over 200,000 cubic metres per second!

Life in the forest

The Amazonian rainforest is one of the planet's most treasured resources. Its vast amount of vegetation takes carbon dioxide out of the air and releases about 20 per cent of the world's oxygen. Despite this there is still a fierce battle to stop people chopping it down, mostly to make way for farming. Many valuable plant and animal species are being lost forever. This is worrying because many of our medicines have been developed from rainforest plants.

▼ A large area of cleared rainforest.

Ghost town

Take a slow boat (see above) from Santarém to visit the ghost town of Fordlândia. It is an abandoned American-style town founded in 1928 by Henry Ford to provide rubber for the tyres of his famous cars. It was a disaster! Ford banned women, alcohol and cigarettes from the town, which sparked a revolt by the workers. Many of his trees died because they were planted too close together. When synthetic rubber was developed the rubber plantations were no longer needed. Fordlândia was abandoned in 1945.

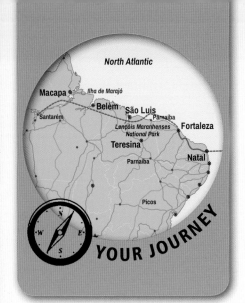

North Atlantic

Macapa
Ilha de Marajó
Belém
Santarém
São Luis
Parnaiba
Fortaleza
Lençóis Maranhenses National Park
Teresina
Natal
Parnaiba
Picos

YOUR JOURNEY

BRAZIL'S BEAUTIFUL BEACHES

Say goodbye to the River Amazon at Santarém. From here you will jump aboard a helicopter, which will whisk you from the heart of the forest to the beautiful beaches of Brazil's northern coast on the Atlantic Ocean. Along the way, the pilot will make a detour to fly over the wonderful Lençóis Maranhenses National Park, (see picture, page 5).

Urban beaches

If you love big cities and beaches, then Fortaleza, the capital of the state of Ceará, is for you. It has 25 km of beaches and is a popular holiday destination for Brazilians. You can enjoy beach parties, scuba diving and eat local food at the beachside restaurants. As well as golden beaches there are quiet fishing villages to explore. Tourism may be one of the key industries in the area, but unfortunately, Fortaleza is not all sunshine and smiles. Brazil has one of the highest crime rates in the world and Fortaleza had the second highest number of murders (2,754) of any city in the world in 2013.

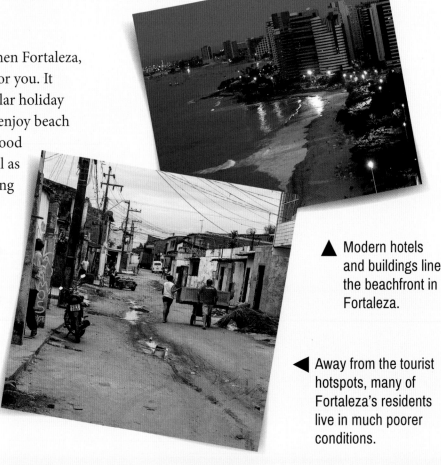

▲ Modern hotels and buildings line the beachfront in Fortaleza.

◀ Away from the tourist hotspots, many of Fortaleza's residents live in much poorer conditions.

▼ Exploring the east coast by beach buggy is a lot of fun!

Beach buggy adventure

You can explore the east coast of Brazil by beach buggy. The trip from Fortaleza to Natal is roughly 750 km and covers nearly a hundred different beaches, many of which remain unspoilt and untouched by tourism. The climate is tropical so expect exceptionally high temperatures and dramatic rainfall. In Natal, visit the *Cajueiro de Pirangi*, the world's biggest cashew tree. It's the size of 70 normal cashew trees!

Island paradise

No visit to the east coast would be complete without a boat trip to the islands of Fernando de Noronha. In 2001 this stunning archipelago's crystal clear, tropical waters and amazing sea life helped it become a UNESCO World Heritage Site. If you go snorkelling, you'll see spinner dolphins and sea turtles.

▲ Delicious lobster are a local speciality.

What's on the menu?

After a day on the beach make sure you sample some of the fresh seafood. Buy squid, shrimp, octopus or lobster at the market and take it to one of the local shacks to be cooked. Other Brazilian dishes to try are *feijoada* (stewed beans and pork) or *Baião de dois* (a rice dish cooked with beans and cheese). In fact, you'll find dishes with beans everywhere!

► Spinner dolphins live in tropical waters.

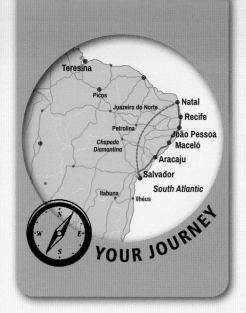

YOUR JOURNEY

BEAUTIFUL BAHIA

From Natal you can catch a bus to explore the state of Bahia. A new international airport opened in Natal in 2014 so you can opt for air travel between Natal and Salvador – however, you're going to miss out on some stunning views!

Natural wonders

The state of Bahia is a state of two halves. It is divided north to south by a chain of eroded, flat-topped mountains called the Chapada Diamantina. '*Chapada*' refers to the sheer cliffs that fall from the table-top mountains and '*Diamantina*' refers to the diamonds that people tried to find there in the 19th century. It's a beautiful region with immense waterfalls and stunning features like the Poço Azul (see right), an underground lake that is lit by the sun through a natural opening.

Sizzling Salvador

Salvador was once the capital of Brazil and it is the place where Africa and South America meet. Also known as the 'City of Happiness', Salvador is one of the oldest cities in all of the Americas. It was first settled in the mid-16th century and quickly became a centre for the slave trade. Consequently, many of its inhabitants are descended from African slaves and the influence of African cultures can be seen in its food, religion, language and music. Brazil is famous for its fantastic carnivals and the one that takes place in Salvador each February is supposed to be the biggest and the best carnival in Brazil!

▶ Carnivals are all about having fun, culture, music and dancing – and they're a great excuse for dressing up!

'Black gold'

There are several types of 'black gold' in Bahia. If you visit the town of Ouro Preto (see below), you will learn about the first kind. *Ouro preto* actually means 'black gold' and refers to the lumps of black iron ore that were mined in the area. These worthless looking lumps actually contained precious gold, which made the town phenomenally rich in the 19th century.

The next 'black gold' is cacao, the main ingredient in chocolate. Bahia is Brazil's main producer and exporter of cacao. Recently cacao trees were devastated by a fungal disease called witches' broom disease. As a result many people in the area lost their jobs. The situation is improving, but there are still fears that lower rates of cacao production could lead to chocolate shortages worldwide.

Another use of the term 'black gold' was for African people transported to the area as slaves. They were called this because of their great value as a cheap source of labour. Of course, the slaves never saw the benefits of their worth, but many others around the world became rich due to their mistreatment.

▲ A gold nugget.

Call of the mountains

If you fancy an adventure why not trek to Cachoeira da Fumaça (see above). The name means 'Smoke Falls' and the cascade gets its name because of the dramatic way the breeze disperses the water on its 340-m descent, creating the impression of smoke.

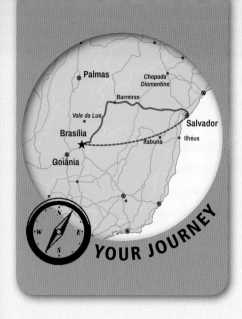

YOUR JOURNEY

BRASÍLIA

The most appropriate way to reach Brasília, the nation's capital, is in a car named after it. The much-loved VW Brasilia was made in the country between 1973 and 1982. Beware though, it's a small car and it takes nearly a day to travel from Salvador into the Brazilian Highlands where the capital lies. You may prefer to fly because that takes just under four hours.

Capital city

Since the 19th century, Brazilian presidents promised that the capital city of the nation would be moved from Rio de Janeiro, on the coast, to a more secure central location. City planning finally got underway in 1956 and the city was officially opened in 1960. It was designed and planned by architect Oscar Niemeyer (1907–2012) and urban planner Lúcio Costa (1902–1998). They came up with a modernist city that has always divided opinion – you'll either love it or hate it!

▼ One way to appreciate the unique design of Brasília is by flying over the city.

Is it a bird?

Brasília is famous for its modern architecture. Make sure you check out the famous crown-like Cathedral of Brasília and the Juscelino Kubitschek Bridge, named after the president who finally moved the capital inland. The city itself has an intriguing design. It is shaped like an aeroplane or a bird, which is best viewed from above. (See if you can spot the 'wings' and 'tail' on page 20.)

◀ The crown-like shape of the cathedral looks especially dramatic when lit up at night.

Excursions into the mountains

Take time to visit the Chapada dos Veadeiros – the highest plateau in Brazil. This national park contains the incredible rock formations of *Vale da Lua* (Valley of the Moon), a surreal landscape that will make you think you're on another planet! If you're quiet and look carefully you may see a giant armadillo. Use your nose and you might detect a maned wolf, also known as a skunk wolf because of the rotten pong it leaves behind.

▶ These rocks in Vale da Lua have been eroded by wind and water into smooth shapes.

Public transport

It may seem strange but there are no rail links to the capital – most railways in the country handle cargo not passengers. There is a good bus service in Brasília and also a metro train but taxi is probably the easiest and safest way to get around the city.

▶ Brasília has a very large bus station in the centre of the city.

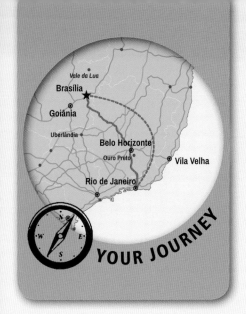

RIO DE JANEIRO

Next, head to Rio de Janeiro, the former capital of Brazil, the country's second largest city and the home of carnival, samba dancing and Sugarloaf Mountain. There are no rail-links to Rio from Brasília, so it's a plane or bus ride again. By air, it takes just under 2 hours; by road it's about 18 hours!

Places to see

Rio's fabulous beaches – Ipanema and Copacabana – are amongst the most famous in the world. Here you will see three Brazilian obsessions in action: beach soccer, beach volleyball and *capoeira* (a fascinating martial art that combines dance and acrobatics). Bikes are seldom used in Brazil because the roads are so dangerous, but Rio does have a bike lending scheme called BikeRio.

If you're not brave enough for cycling, you could ride the historic Santa Teresa tramway from the city centre to a residential area of the city called Santa Teresa. One of the highlights of the journey is a ride over the 45-metre-high Carioca Aqueduct. However you get around the city, make sure you visit the amazing Niterói Contemporary Art Museum, designed by Oscar Niemeyer.

▼ Beach soccer is a common sight on Rio's Beaches.

Rich and poor

Although Brazil is considered a wealthy country, with the seventh biggest economy in the world, the riches are not evenly divided, and some of the wealthiest people on the planet live close to some of the poorest. One of the wealthiest neighbourhoods, Leblon, is only 3 km from one of the poorest, Rocinha. Rocinha began as a *favela* (slum) and is home to over 600,000 people. The oldest favela in Brazil was built by homeless soldiers returning from the Canudos civil war at the end of the 19th century. They named their new home the Favela after Favela Hill in Canudos.

▲ Rocinha is the biggest favela in Rio.

Christ the Redeemer

One of the most iconic sites in Rio is Christ the Redeemer, a 30-metre-high statue created in 1922 by the French sculptor Paul Landowski. It stands on top of Corcovado Mountain and is a great place to see incredible views of the city and Guanabara Bay.

▶ The statue of Christ the Redeemer.

Sugarloaf Mountain

Another iconic feature of Rio is the curiously-shaped Sugarloaf Mountain. It rises 396 m above the city and gets its name because it looks like a sugarloaf – the old-fashioned way of presenting sugar, as a cone, before sugar lumps and granulated sugar were introduced. It is a granite monolith that formed underground and then softer earth around it eroded away over time to leave an impressive peak.

▲ The distinctive shape of Sugarloaf Mountain.

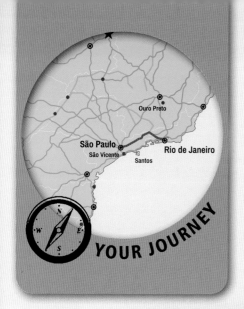

YOUR JOURNEY

SÃO PAULO

It's time to head off to the world's largest city south of the equator: São Paulo. It is often called the 'locomotive of Brazil' because it (and the area around it) is so important to the country's economy. The important industries in the region are coffee, cane sugar and cars.

▼ São Paulo is the most densely populated area of Brazil.

'Coffee pot of the world'

Coffee was first smuggled into Brazil in 1727 from neighbouring French Guiana. That secret stash of coffee beans developed into a massive industry, and Brazil became known as 'the coffee pot of the world'. Brazil's environment and subtropical climate are ideal for growing coffee plants and, as the industry developed, millions of people flocked to the region to find work on plantations and in factories. At one time Brazil supplied 80 per cent of the world's coffee. Today, it is still the largest producer, providing about 30 per cent of the planet's total.

▼ Coffee beans.

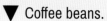

Super sugarcane

Brazil is also the largest sugarcane producer in the world. Like coffee, sugarcane is not indigenous to Brazil, but it grows well in São Paulo's climate. Sugar is not just a foodstuff as Brazil is at the forefront of technology to turn sugarcane into a fuel called ethanol. This biofuel can power cars and other machines. In 2013 Brazil was the second highest producer of ethanol in the world (second to the USA) and about 60 per cent of this was produced near São Paulo.

'The São Paulo taxi driver'

The Formula 1 racing driver, Ayrton Senna (see below), was nicknamed 'the São Paulo taxi driver', supposedly because he was as ruthless on the track as the taxi drivers are around his home city. He is considered by many to be one of the greatest drivers of all time. He won the drivers' championship three times and the Brazilian Grand Prix – held here in his hometown – twice. He died while competing in the San Marino Grand Prix in 1994.

Brazil's booming car use

In the past ten years, the number of cars on Brazil's roads has risen by more than 100 per cent. Gridlock and rising pollution levels are a serious problem in Brazil's major cities, including São Paulo. The government has introduced tougher restrictions on cars in cities and is promoting non-motorised transport. To reduce pollution, cars have to be more energy efficient, too. Brazil leads the way in this field; cars have been running on a blend of oil and ethanol for over 30 years.

▲ Gridlocked roads are a result of the rise in car-ownership.

SÃO BERNARDO DO CAMPO TO SANTOS

In São Paulo you can hire a classic VW type 2 campervan, also known as 'the Kombi', which you'll drive on the trip to Santos on the Atlantic coast. Your first stop is the very last place the vans were made: São Bernardo do Campo, an area in the south of São Paulo's massive urban sprawl.

Germany v. Brazil

The Brazilian love affair with the German Volkswagen (VW) car began in the 1950s. Imported VW cars were highly desired, but very expensive. The government charged high taxes to import foreign cars, so the German company set up a Brazilian car factory in São Bernardo do Campo.

This gave people in the area jobs and provided Brazilian motorists with cheaper VW Beetles (known here as the '*Fusca*') and campervans that they loved. Soon they started to make their own Brazilian models like the VW Brasilia and they became one of the biggest car manufacturers in the country. Sadly, the last campervans rolled off the production line in Brazil in December 2013.

▶ A classic Volkswagen Kombi.

São Vicente

Santos is Brazil's biggest and most important port. Goods from all over the word arrive and leave from here on enormous container ships. The next town along is São Vicente and this is where most of the workers of Santos live. São Vicente is notable for being the first Portuguese settlement in Brazil. It was founded in 1532 and the only surviving feature from that era is the Biquinha de Anchieta – a fountain that was the town's original water supply.

▼ An empty container ship waits to be loaded in the port of Santos.

O Rei Pelé and the *Jogo Bonito* (The King Pelé and the Beautiful Game)

Football is the most popular sport in Brazil and the national team have won the World Cup five times – more than any other nation. So where better to explore Brazil's footballing heritage than at the Pelé Museum, in the town of FC Santos, the football club where Pelé's playing brought him to the nation's attention. Pelé regularly tops the lists of the world's greatest footballers. He scored a whopping 77 goals in 92 matches for his country. He played in four World Cups for Brazil and won three of them! He is the only player to accomplish this.

▲ Pelé posing with young players at the opening of the Pelé Museum.

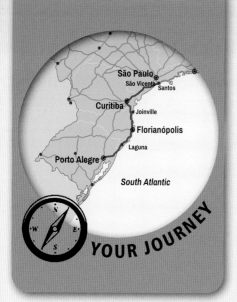

YOUR JOURNEY

SOUTHERN BRAZIL

The south of Brazil has it all – buzzing cities, gorgeous beaches and snowy mountain ranges. Wrap up as you head further south in your campervan because the temperature dips – sometimes as low as freezing point!

Eco-citizens of Curitiba

Like many newly developed cities in Brazil, Curitiba is famed worldwide for its clever urban planning. You won't need the campervan to move about this city, its innovative bus-based public transport system is so quick and successful that many of the Curitibanos prefer to leave their cars at home. As a result, the city has one of the lowest rates of pollution in the whole country. Citizens of Curitiba can also congratulate themselves on their recycling – an estimated 70 per cent of the city's waste is recycled. Since the 1970s innovative programmes like exchanging recyclable goods for surplus food, free transport or even tickets to the football or shows has encouraged people from all ages and backgrounds to recycle.

▶ Even Curitiba's bus stops are slick and modern.

Back at the beach

At Curitiba jump aboard a bus to Florianópolis to sample some more beach action before you leave the country. Brazil has 7,491 km of coastline and some of the best beaches in the world, but Florianópolis is arguably the best if you love to surf. It has 42 beaches with varying levels of difficulty to suit beginners or experts and, it has good surfing waves all year round.

Lending a helping fin

Leave your surfboard behind and take a two-hour drive to Laguna to witness an extraordinary example of cooperation between humans and animals. For several generations, bottlenose dolphins in the area have been helping the local fishermen to catch fish by herding them into nets and signalling to the men when to haul in the catch.

Visit a museum

Fans of modern architecture must visit the Oscar Niemeyer Museum in Curitiba. Shaped like a giant eye, (see below) it was designed by the great man and finished in 2002, when he was 95.

Head to the hills

Your journey is nearly complete as you approach Porto Alegre – the place where you first landed. Before you say goodbye to Brazil you should take time to visit São Joaquim to see the beautiful snow-capped Santa Catarina mountains. Gazing at these glorious peaks will ensure that you never again think of Brazil as just sand, soccer and samba.

▼ Ring-tailed coatis (a relative of the raccoon) live in the Santa Catarina mountains.

GLOSSARY

armadillo
A mammal with a tough, leathery, armoured skin.

aqueduct
A bridge or channel designed to carry water.

archipelago
A group of islands.

assassinate
To murder someone for political reasons.

biodiversity
A wide range of animal and plant species.

campaign
Organised actions, such as posting leaflets, holding marches, to try to get something done.

carnival
A celebration or festival usually involving some sort of street procession, often with music, dancing and specially-designed costumes.

ceramic
Something made of clay and hardened by heat.

continent
A large continuous land mass.

deforestation
The destruction of a large area of trees.

disperse
To spread out or scatter.

desert
A place with very little rain.

diverse
Having a great deal of variety.

endangered
An animal, plant or other living thing at risk of extinction.

eroded
When something is worn away, usually by wind or water.

estimate
A guess based on a rough calculation.

extinction
To die out.

gridlock
When there is so much traffic that vehicles can't move.

hemisphere
Half of a sphere or half of the world.

hydroelectric dam
A man-made construction that uses the power of water flow to make electricity.

import
To bring goods into a country.

indigenous
Living or occurring naturally in a particular place.

innovative
New and original ideas or creations.

iron ore
The raw material that iron comes from.

latex
A natural form of rubber from the sap of the rubber tree.

manufacturers
People who make things on a large scale, often in factories.

marmoset
A small long-tailed monkey.

modernist
A movement in the arts and architecture that started in the early 20th century that aimed to produce modern works different from classical designs from the past.

monsoon
The rainy season.

national park
A part of the countryside that is protected by the government.

obelisk
A pillar used as a monument.

piranha
A meat-eating fish that swims and feeds in large groups.

plateau
A level of high, flat ground.

recline
To lean or lie back.

reservoir
A large store of something, usually water. A water reservoir looks like a large lake.

slave
Someone owned by someone else and often forced to work for no pay.

subtropical
The climate of regions just above and below the tropics.

sugarcane
A tall grass that contains a source of sugar.

sustainable
A way of not wasting natural resources.

tributaries
Rivers that flow into larger rivers.

tropical
The climate of the regions around the equator up to the Tropic of Cancer and the Tropic of Capricorn.

UNESCO
Part of the United Nations. UNESCO World Heritage sites are places that are protected because they have such a high cultural value.

urban planner
Someone who designs a city layout and environment.

vaccination
To protect someone against a dangerous disease by giving them a weaker version of it, so their body can fight it more efficiently.

yellow fever
A tropical disease caught from mosquitos that affects the liver and kidneys.

BOOKS TO READ

Countries Around Our World: Brazil by Marion Morrison (Raintree, 2012)

DK Eyewitness Travel Guide: Brazil (DK Eyewitness Travel, 2012)

In Our World: Brazil by Edward Parker (Franklin Watts, 2012)

Lonely Planet: Brazil Travel Guide (Loncly Planet, 2013)

My Holiday in: Brazil by Jane Bingham (Wayland, 2014)

The Real Brazil by Paul Mason (Franklin Watts, 2014)

River Adventures: Amazon by Paul Manning (FranklinWatts, 2014)

The Rough Guide to Brazil by Clemmy Manzo and Kiki Deere (Rough Guides, 2014)

Rainforest Rough Guide By Paul Mason (A & C Black, 2010)

WEBSITES

Check out YouTube for films by other travellers to Brazil. As well as taking a look at the sights and sounds of many of the places mentioned in this book, there are travel tips and the top places to visit. You can subscribe to Hey Nadine and follow her journey through Brazil in 2013 when she visited places like Rio de Janeiro, Salvador and the Amazon rainforest.

https://www.youtube.com/watch?v=876kwq5Myxg https://www.youtube.com/watch?v=70R8llNmf2k

Also on YouTube is the Brazil Travel Guide by Expoza, which is an informative guide to the nation and its fascinating history, it's also a great way to see the sights before even setting foot in the country:

https://www.youtube.com/watch?v=lshNdiTvNMI

The VisitBrasil website is packed full of practical advice for travel as well as information about all the major tourist and not-so touristy destinations. The website has great photographs and it will help you plan your perfect trip to Brazil:

http://www.visitbrasil.com/en/

As well as books, Lonely Planet has inspirational, informative websites devoted to travel. The Brazil website is so colourful and visually exciting, don't be surprised if Brazil goes to number one in your list of dream destinations:

http://www.lonelyplanet.com/brazil

Rough Guide also have a great website, which will help you plan where to go, what to do, how to get around and practical info for your trip to Brazil:

http://www.roughguides.com/destinations/south-america/brazil/

Note to parents and teachers:
Every effort has been made by the Publishers to ensure that the websites in this book are suitable for children, that they are of the highest educational value, and that they contain no inappropriate or offensive material. However, because of the nature of the Internet, it is impossible to guarantee that the contents of these sites will not be altered. We strongly advise that Internet access is supervised by a responsible adult.

INDEX

Amazon rainforest 11–15
Argentina 8–9

beach soccer 22
beach volleyball 22
beaches 4, 16–17, 22, 28–29
Bolivia 12
Brasília 20–22
brazilwood 4

Cabral, Pedro 4
cacao (cocoa/chocolate) 19
Cachoeira da Fumaça 19
Campo Grande 10
capoeira 22
carnivals 18, 22
cars 15, 20, 24–26
Chapada Diamantina 18
Chapada dos Veadeiros 21
Christ the Redeemer statue 23
climate 5, 12, 17, 24–25
coffee 24
Copacabana 22
Costa, Lúcio 20
cowboys 11
crime 16
Cuiabá 10–12
Curitiba 28–29

deforestation 4, 15

ethanol 25

farming 13, 15, 19
favelas 23
Fernando de Noronha 17
Florianópolis 29
food 16–17
football 4, 8, 22, 27–29
Fordlândia 15
Formula 1 25

Fortaleza 16–17

gold 11, 19
Guaíra Falls 9

hydroelectricity 7

Iguaçu Falls 8
Iguaçu National Park 9
Interoceanic Highway 13
Ipanema 22
Itaipu Hydroelectric Dam 9

Laguna 29
Landowski, Paul 23
languages 5
Lençóis Maranhenses National
    Park 5, 16
logging 4, 13, 15

Manaus 5, 14
map 6–7
Mendes, Chico 13
mining 19
mountains 13, 18, 21–23, 28–29

Natal 16–18
national parks 5, 9–11, 16, 21
Niemeyer, Oscar 20, 22
Niterói Contemporary Art
    Museum 22

Oscar Niemeyer Museum 29
Ouro Preto 19

Pantanal, the 10–11
Paraguay 9
Paraná River 9
Pelé Museum 27
peoples 5, 13
Poço Azul 18

population 4–5
Porto Alegre 8, 29
Portugal 4, 27

recycling 28
Rio Branco 12–13
Rio de Janeiro 20, 22–23
River Acre 12
River Amazon 14–16
River Negro 5
River Tapajós 14
Roosevelt, Eleanor 8
rubber industry 12–15

Salvador 18, 20
samba 22, 29
Santa Teresa historic tramway 22
Santarém 14–16
Santos 26–27
São Bernardo do Campo 26
São Joaquim 29
São Paulo 24–26
São Vicente 27
Senna, Ayrton 25
slave trade 18–19
sugarcane 24–25
Sugarloaf Mountain 22–23

Teatro Amazonas 14
travel tips 5
tribes, uncontacted 13

Volkswagen 20, 26

waterfalls 8–9, 18–19
wildlife 9, 11, 14–15, 17, 21, 29
World Cup 8, 27

Xapuri 12–13